A First Look at Art
Weather

Ruth Thomson

Chrysalis Children's Books

First published in the UK in 2005 by

Chrysalis Children's Books

An imprint of Chrysalis Books Group Plc

The Chrysalis Building, Bramley Road

London W10 6SP

ISBN 1 84458 200 0

British Library Cataloguing in Publication Data for this book is available from the British Library.

Editorial manager *Joyce Bentley*
Project manager *Rasha Elsaeed*
Editor *Susie Brooks*
Designers *Rachel Hamdi, Holly Mann*
Picture researcher *Claire Gouldstone*
Photographer *Jerry Moeran*
Consultant *Erika Langmuir, formerly Head of Education, The National Gallery, London, UK*

The author and publishers would like to thank the following people for their contributions to this book: Penny Stevenson and pupils at St Mary's School, Henley-on-Thames; Jacqueline Hart, Bronwyn Macdonald and pupils at St Hugh's School, Ware; Claudia Celder.

Printed in China

Typography *Natascha Frensch*
Read Regular, Read Smallcaps and Read Space; European Community Design Registration 2003 and Copyright © Natascha Frensch 2001-2004 Read Medium, **Read Black** and *Read Slanted* Copyright © Natascha Frensch 2003-2004

READ™ is a revolutionary new typeface that will enchance children's understanding through clear, easily recognisable character shapes. With its evenly spaced and carefully designed characters, READ™ will help children at all stages to improve their literacy skills and is ideal for young readers, reluctant readers and especially children with dyslexia.

Picture acknowledgements

All reasonable efforts have been made to ensure the reproduction of content has been done with the consent of copyright owners. If you are aware of any unintentional omissions please contact the publishers directly so that any necessary corrections may be made for future editions.
Front cover Art Institute of Chicago/Gustave Caillebotte, French 1848-1894, 'Paris Street; Rainy Day', 1877, oil on canvas, 212.2x276.2cm, Charles H. and Mary F. S. Worcester Collection, 1964.336. 4 'Tiger in a Tropical Storm (Surprised!)' by Henri Rousseau © The National Gallery, London. 5 The Butler Institute of American Art/Burchfield, Charles. 'Late Winter Radiance', 1961-62, watercolour on paper, 44x26.5cm. Courtesy of the Butler Institute of American Art, Youngstown, Oh. 6 © Tate, London 2004/David Hockney 'A Bigger Splash' 1967 96x96cm. © David Hockney. 7 Reunion des Musées Nationaux/ © Photo RMN - Hérve Lewandowski. 10-11 Hendrik Averkamp, 'Winter Landscape with Ice Skaters', 77x132cm, c1608. © Rijksmuseum, Amsterdam. 14-15 Art Institute of Chicago/ Gustave Caillebotte, French 1848-1894, 'Paris Street; Rainy Day', 1877, oil on canvas, 212.2x276.2cm, Charles H. and Mary F. S. Worcester Collection, 1964.336. 18-19 Private Collection © ADAGP, Paris and DACS, London 2004. 22 Reunion des Musées Nationaux/© Photo RMN - Harry Bréjat. 23 Fitzwilliam Museum, University of Cambridge. 26, 27 © William Heath Robinson/Permission granted by the estate of Mrs J C Robinson and Pollinger Limited.

Contents

Whatever the weather 4

Sunny days 6

Sun and snow 8

    CRISP COLLAGES 8

    SANDY STRIPS 8

    WINTRY WHITE 9

Fun on the ice 10

Seasonal scenes 12

    WINTER WONDERLAND 12

    ALL SEASONS 12

    BLOWING BRANCHES 13

    SNOW SHOW 13

Walking in the rain 14
Rainy days 16
   WATERY HAZE 16
   UNDER UMBRELLAS 16
   RAINY REFLECTIONS 17

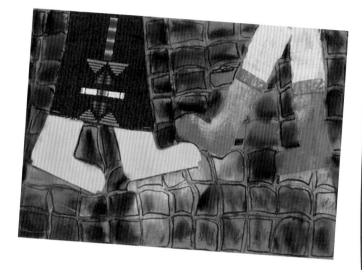

Feeling the heat 18
Red-hot 20
   SIZZLING STRIPES 20
   BLAZING LIGHT 21

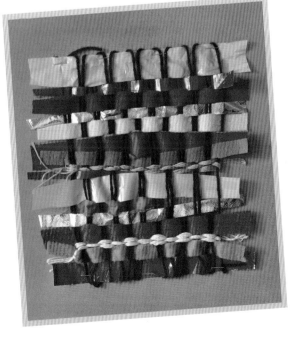

Blowing in the wind 22
Windy works 24
   WHOOSH! 24
   WINDBLOWN WALKERS 25

Wacky weather 26
Model machines 28
   SNOW SCOOPER 28
   CLOTHES CHOOSER 29

Artists and answers 30

Glossary and index 32

WHATEVER THE WEATHER

Creating scenes showing wind, rain or sunlight is a challenge for artists. Wind is invisible, rain is colourless and light can change from moment to moment. In this book we'll explore how artists have depicted different kinds of weather. You'll learn about their ideas and techniques. There are also questions to help you look at the works in detail, and art projects for you to try out.

◉ *You'll find answers to the questions and information about the artists on pages 30-31.*

Arty tips

✭ Look out for Arty tips boxes that suggest handy techniques and materials to use in your own work.

Picture hunt

✭ Picture hunt boxes suggest other artists and artworks that you might like to look at.

Tiger in a Tropical Storm (Surprised!), *Henri Rousseau, 1891 (130 x 162 cm)*

A sudden storm

Some painters try to capture on canvas exactly what they see. Others paint imaginary scenes, such as the one on the left by Henri Rousseau.

Rousseau made up this image of a violent storm from sketches of plants and animals that he drew at the Botanical Gardens in Paris. Flashes of lightning quiver in the dark, thundery sky. The leaves, branches and grass are all bent in one direction, as if blown by a strong wind. The whole picture has been covered with slanting streaks of grey and white glaze, to indicate heavy, tropical rain.

Wondrous weather

Charles Burchfield was amazed by nature in all weathers. In his picture of a forest in winter *(above right)*, he tried to express his sense of wonder. He created a magical, glittery scene to convey the power, beauty and endlessness of the sun and seasons.

Late Winter Radiance
Charles Burchfield
1961-62
(44 x 26.5 cm)

SUNNY DAYS

A Bigger Splash, *David Hockney, 1967 (243.8 x 243.8 cm)*

These two paintings both show sunny weather, but at different times of year. Look at the contrasts between them.

◉ *What difference do you notice between the ranges of colours the artists used?*

◉ *What colours did they use for shadows?*

Plunge in

In Hockney's picture above, we see a cool blue swimming pool on a hot, cloudless day. The cheerful yellow diving board has been carefully angled, as if inviting us to dive in.

The Magpie, *Claude Monet, 1868-1869 (89 x 130 cm)*

Creating a splash

Our eye is drawn to smudges, drizzles and spots of white paint in the middle of the pool. They create movement, while the rest of the scene is calm.

◉ *What do these marks indicate?*

Still surroundings

Hockney made the setting seem still by using bold horizontal and vertical lines for the house, trees and pool-side. He used a roller to paint everything – except the splash – very smoothly.

◉ *Why do you think he did this?*

Winter colours

Monet's painting (*above*) is set early on a winter's morning. The narrow range of pale colours creates a feeling of soft, weak sunlight and the crisp chill of snow. The trees and hedges are laden with thick dabs of cool grey and blue as well as white. By contrast, two bright chimneys hint at the cosy warmth inside the house.

◉ *How can you tell that it is morning?*
◉ *Why did Monet include the magpie on the gate? Hide it with your finger. How does the picture look without it?*

SUN AND SNOW

Crisp collages

Make a collage of a hot place. Cut out
coloured paper shapes and glue them
on to card.

◉ Keep the shapes bold and simple.

◉ Use strong, contrasting colours to
make your picture zing.

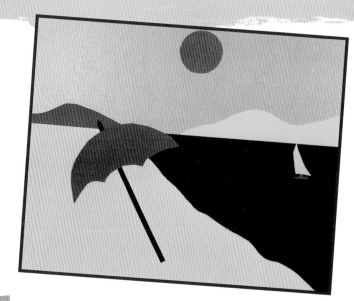

Chris, aged 10

Harry, aged 10

George, aged 10

Sandy strips

Glue overlapping strips of torn tissue paper
on to paper to make a beach scene.

Joshua, aged 10

◉ If you want to add more
texture, spread glue on the paper
and sprinkle over some fine sand.

Charlie, aged 9

Wintry white

Paint a wintry landscape with snow-covered trees. Like Monet, use a mixture of pale colours for the snow and sky. Blues and greys create a chilly feel – artists call them 'cool colours'.

Picture hunt

✧ Enjoy some of Hockney's other Californian scenes, such as **Santa Monica Boulevard, Canyon Painting** and **A Lawn Being Sprinkled**.

✧ Compare how other artists paint snowy scenes with trees, such as **Effect of Snow near Pontoise** by Camille Pissarro and **The Watering Place at Marly-le-Roi** by Alfred Sisley.

Danny, aged 10

◉ Sponge-paint a background.

◉ Add trees, houses, fences and other details.

◉ Include shadows to show where the sun is shining from.

George, aged 10

Arty tips

✧ Look outside at shadows and where they fall in relation to the sun. Notice how they are different lengths at different times of day.

✧ Explore how white things, such as snow, change in different lights. Look for other colours in the whiteness.

Jonathon, aged 10

Hendrik Avercamp was famous for painting action-packed winter scenes of his home town in Holland. This one is typical, showing people out and about on the chilly frozen river.

The picture conjures up a very cold feeling. We see bare, spiky trees, heavy, grey sky, and ice thick enough to carry the weight of horse-drawn sleighs. The slippery ice shines with reflections.

Dozens of details

People rich and poor, young and old, working and playing are all seen here. Unusually, most have their backs to us.

◉ *Discover:*
- *a man tying on his skate*
- *a fallen skater*
- *a ragged man begging*
- *two horse-drawn sleighs*
- *men playing kolf (a game like ice hockey)*
- *a sign for the Half-Moon Brewery*
- *a big hole in the ice (for the brewery to draw water for beer-making)*
- *a man pushing a sled*
- *a man on a horse*
- *two men with fishing rods*
- *three pairs of skaters holding hands*
- *a reed-cutter carrying a large bundle of reeds*
- *a man with a fishing net*
- *a woman carrying a pair of buckets.*

Fading out

Notice how the people, trees and buildings along the river become smaller, less detailed and paler as your eye follows them into the distance. The fading colours also create a sense of hazy, cloudy weather.

SEASONAL SCENES

Winter wonderland

Use oil pastels or wax crayons to create a busy scene of people having fun outside in winter.

◉ If you want to suggest distance, make some trees and figures smaller and higher up on the page.

◉ Use dotty marks for falling snow.

Isabella, aged 8

Ghislaine, aged 8

◉ If you use blue or grey paper, leave some of the paper showing through. This will help create an icy atmosphere.

◉ Give people brightly coloured clothes to make them stand out.

Picture hunt

✧ Look at other busy icy scenes by Avercamp, such as **The Delights of Winter, Frozen River, A Winter Scene with Skaters near a Castle, Winter Landscape with Frozen River and Figures** and **A Scene of the Ice near a Town.**

Uzair, aged 8

All seasons

Try making pictures of people outside in other seasons, too.
- ◉ Choose typical activities and colours for each time of year.
- ◉ Notice how the trees change.

SPRING   Alexandra, aged 9   SUMMER   Lucinda, aged 8   AUTUMN   Isabella, aged 9

Blowing branches

Paint a picture of a bare tree in winter with its dark, spiky branches.
- ◉ Paint a background of ground and sky.
- ◉ Put a blob of watery paint on the paper and, using a drinking straw, gently blow the wet paint into the shape of a tree with knobbly branches. Tilt the paper to help direct the flow of paint.

Toby, aged 9

Snow show

- ◉ Blow-paint a tree on a blank page. Let it dry.
- ◉ Draw around it with a white candle tip. Add snowy scribbles on the ground and in the sky.
- ◉ Brush the ground and sky with watery paint. The waxy snow marks will show through.

Thomas, aged 8

Arty tips

- ✿ Blow-painting can be messy, so cover your work surface with newspaper before you start.
- ✿ Use quite watery paint for blow-painting.
- ✿ Remember to remove the straw from your mouth and take breaths between blows.

WALKING IN THE RAIN

Many artists have been interested in painting scenes of everyday life. Caillebotte was one of them. He lived in Paris at a time when the city had recently been rebuilt with wide streets, lined with tall apartment buildings. This huge picture is a snapshot of a quiet, ordinary moment on the streets of Paris, one dull, drizzly day.

Signs of rain

There are several signs here of wet weather, apart from the obvious clue of open umbrellas. The wet cobblestones glisten gently and the shadows cast by the walkers and the lamppost seem to shimmer.

◉ *What main colours has Caillebotte used to suggest it is a rainy day?*
◉ *What clues give the impression that it is chilly as well as wet?*

Sense of space

Caillebotte has created an unreal wide-angle view of the streets to give a feeling of great space and distance. He has also set the people in zig-zags across the picture, so our eye is drawn into the scene.

◉ *How do you think the people are feeling?*

G. Caillebotte 1877

Paris Street, Rainy Day, *Gustave Caillebotte, 1877 (212 x 276 cm)*

RAINY DAYS

Watery haze

Use water-soluble pencils to create interesting rainy-day effects.

Draw the outlines of a picture in ink or felt-tipped pen.

Colour in the scene with water-soluble pencils.

Using a brush and clean water, paint over the colours to blend and soften them.

Under umbrellas

Create a picture of people walking along a city street in a downpour.

◉ Draw the outlines of the figures first.

◉ Include features of a city – buildings, pavements, street lights and bus stops.

◉ Colour them with water-soluble pencils.

Edward, aged 9

◉ Wash over the colours with a wet brush to create a damp, drizzly feel.

Kathryn, aged 9

Callum, aged 9

Rainy reflections

Make a collage of someone walking across a glistening wet pavement.

◉ Use chalk pastels to cover a sheet of paper with cobblestones.

◉ Cut out a pair of colourful rubber boots from shiny, sticky-backed plastic. Stick them in place.

◉ Cut out a skirt or some trousers from fabric. Glue these in place.

Arty tips

✿ Give the cobblestones depth and texture by building up layers of several colours, one on top of the other.

✿ Use textured paper if you want an uneven surface of colour.

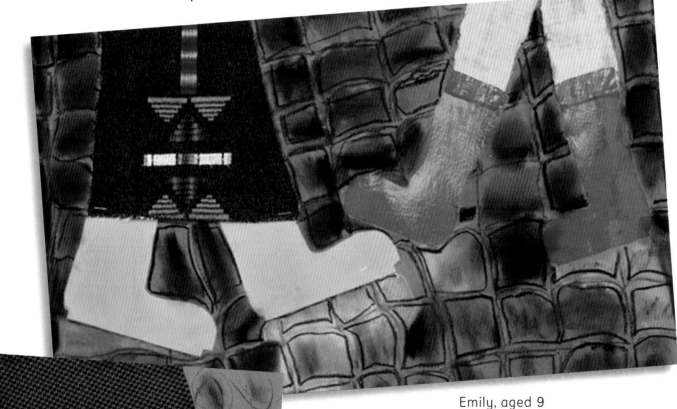

Emily, aged 9

Joelle, aged 9

◉ Draw reflections in a similar colour to the boots, but paler. Blur their outlines if you want them to appear to shimmer.

Picture hunt

✿ Look at pictures which depict rain very differently, such as **Sudden Rain on Mount Tempo** by Gakutei; **Rain, Steam and Speed** by J. M. W. Turner; **Night Equinox** by Charles Burchfield and **Tiger in a Tropical Storm (Surprised!)** by Henri Rousseau (see page 4).

FEELING THE HEAT

Have you ever seen bright red sand, a green and yellow sky or pink mountains? Derain painted this beach in France not the way it looked, but how it *felt* on a sizzling, hot summer's day.

Summer sensation

Derain's vivid, but unreal, colours express the feeling of scorching sand, the effect of hot, dazzling sunlight, and the sparkle of a calm, rippling sea.

◉ *What sort of brushstrokes suggest that the water is rippling?*
◉ *Why might Derain have left parts of the bare canvas showing?*

Hot hues

Notice the colours that Derain has used to paint the figures, sweltering in the sun. Some are red all over; the two on the right have fiery faces and one has a bright yellow body. Shades of red, yellow and orange are known to artists as 'hot colours'.

◉ *How did Derain make the figure sitting on the right stand out?*

Boats in the Port of Collioure
André Derain, 1905 (72 x 91 cm)

RED-HOT

Sizzling stripes

Make a weaving in burning colours that remind you of a scorching day.

◉ First make a loom. Snip V-shaped notches along the top and bottom of a cardboard rectangle. (You may need adult help.)

◉ Make a knot in the end of a long length of wool. Run the wool up and down one side of the cardboard, looping it over the notches at each end, until you have covered the loom. These threads are called the warp.

V-shaped notches

the warp

Lucy, aged 8

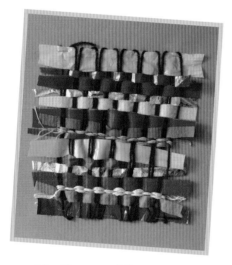

Martha, aged 8

Thomas, aged 8

Harvey, aged 7

◉ Cut colourful strips of fabric, just a little longer than the width of your loom.

◉ Starting at the top of the loom, weave a strip first under and then over the warp. Then weave a second strip first over and then under the warp. Continue weaving alternately like this, until you reach the end of the loom.

Arty tips

✥ Weave with a mixture of materials, such as soft felt, shiny ribbon, raffia, patterned fabric, thick wool, binding tape, coloured cellophane and metallic paper.

✥ Once you have finished, carefully unhook your weaving from the loom. Then stick it on to some contrasting coloured card to display it.

20

Blazing light

Make a see-through picture in hot, bright colours to cheer you up on a gloomy day.

◉ Tear some tissue paper into all sorts of odd-shaped pieces. Use a variety of hot colours.

◉ Cut a square or rectangle of clear cellophane.

◉ Arrange your pieces, overlapping some of them, on the cellophane.

◉ Glue the pieces in place, using PVA glue

◉ Tape your picture on to a window or a glass door, so light can shine through it and make it glow.

Edward, aged 7, and Aubrey, aged 8

Picture hunt

✧ Look at some other very hot landscapes, such as: **The Turning Road, L'Estaque** by André Derain; **Landscape at Ceret** by Juan Gris; **The Artist on the Road to Tarascon** and **The Siesta** by Vincent van Gogh; **Wild Poppies near Argenteuil** by Monet; **The Red Buoy** by Paul Signac; **Figures on the Seashore** and **Sicilian Landscape: View of Agrigente** by Nicholas de Staël.

BLOWING IN THE WIND

Eriji in Suruga Province (A Sudden Gust of Wind), *Hokusai, c1831 (28.1 x 25.4 cm)*

Wind is invisible and constantly on the move, so how can artists depict it in a flat, still artwork?

Windswept walk

Hokusai's print is of a windy moment frozen in time, where the effects of a sudden gust can be clearly seen. As the trees sway, some of their leaves scatter. People struggle to stay upright as they make their way along the path, holding on tightly to their hats. Everything is shown with a firm outline and in crisp detail.

◉ *How do people's clothes emphasise how hard the wind is blowing?*

◉ *Where is the wind blowing from? How can you tell?*

Blown away

Notice how the trail of papers leads your eye from left to right and up into the air, showing the path of the wind. This diagonal line gives the picture a strong sense of movement.

◉ *What else in the picture is windblown?*

◉ *What feels still and unaffected by the force of the wind?*

Fleeting flurry

In the picture below, we capture a glimpse of a blustery landscape. The bushes, trees and grass seem to ripple in the wind. The puffy clouds appear to sweep before our eyes and the blue sky makes the air feel fresh and clear.

Moving marks

Renoir, the artist, overlapped and blended dabs of paint to give a fuzzy, smudged effect of movement. It is similar to a photo taken with a shaky hand, where details merge together.

Shivery shapes

To emphasise wind rushing through the trees and bushes, Renoir blurred their outlines. He painted some with feathery brushstrokes and others with blotchy ones. Look closely at the direction of the brushstrokes.

◉ *Where is the wind coming from?*
◉ *Why did Renoir add white patches in the foreground? Cover them to see the difference it makes without them.*
◉ *Compare the two pictures. Which do you think gives the most effective impression of a windy moment?*

The Gust of Wind, *Pierre-Auguste Renoir, c1872 (52 x 82 cm)*

WINDY WORKS

Whoosh!

Use soft chalk pastels to create a wild and windy landscape.

◉ Make diagonal strokes or swirls, all in the same direction, to show which way the wind is blowing.

Max, aged 11

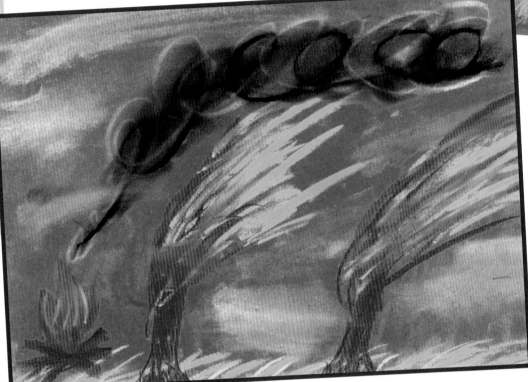

Tom, aged 11

◉ Overlap different colours to give a blurred effect of movement.

◉ If you want colours to blend or spread, smudge them gently with your finger.

Picture hunt

✧ Find other paintings of windswept landscapes, such as Van Gogh's **Wheatfield with Crows**, Cézanne's **Tall Trees at the Jas de Bouffan** or **September Wind and Rain** by Charles Burchfield.

✧ Look at other pictures of windblown people, such as **Sudden Rainstorm at Shono** by Hiroshige or Claude Monet's **Woman with a Parasol – Madame Monet and her Son.**

Tim, aged 11

Windblown walkers

Make a model of a windblown figure.

◉ Sketch how people look when they are windblown. Notice how they stand and what happens to their hair and clothes.

Jessica, aged 11

Tom, aged 11

◉ Twist thin wire into the shape of a windblown person. Make circles for the head and body.

◉ Attach the feet to a block of wood, so the figure stands up. You may need adult help with this.

◉ Stuff the head and body with crumpled newspaper.

◉ Use mod-roc, or strips of newspaper dipped in PVA glue, to cover the whole model.

◉ When the sculpture is dry, paint it all over.

Max, aged 11

Arty tips

✫ Keep the shape simple. Don't model hands, feet or a face in detail.

✫ Twist on separate bent wire strands for windblown hair.

✫ Add extra features, such as a waving scarf or an umbrella, to create a feeling of action.

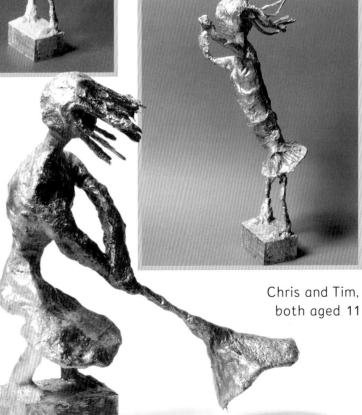
Chris and Tim, both aged 11

Jessica, aged 11

What Shall I Put On?, *William Heath Robinson, 1934*

A New Snow-plough for
Clearing a Footpath after
a Heavy Fall
William Heath Robinson
1934

Heath Robinson was
nicknamed 'The Gadget
King' because of his
humorous illustrations
of absurd inventions.
Two are shown here.

Weather wear

The invention in the
picture on the left is
designed to tell people
what kind of clothes to
wear, according to the
weather. A buoy bobs
up or down in a tiny
water tank. Its arrow
points to 'wet' or 'dry',
depending how much
rain has dripped into
the tank from the
funnel on the roof. As
the weathervane moves
in the wind, it powers
two cogs. These, in turn,
move an arrow which
points to the type of
clothes to wear.

◉ *How does Heath
Robinson show
the rain collecting?*

W. HEATH
ROBINSON

Snow to go

Do you think this snow-
clearing machine could
work? Examine it closely.

◉ *What powers the broom
that sweeps the snow?*
◉ *What makes the snow
scooper turn?*

◉ *What happens to the
scoops of snow?*
◉ *What are the people
on the platform doing?*
◉ *Why is there a roller on
the back of the machine?*
◉ *How does the driver
warn that he's coming?*

MODEL MACHINES

Snow scooper

Design your own snow-clearing machine. Think about these things before you start:

- How will your machine move through deep snow?
- How will it collect snow?
- What will happen to the snow once it is collected?
- Will it have lights, so it can work at night? Where will these fit?
- How many people will be needed to operate the machine?
- Where will they sit or stand?

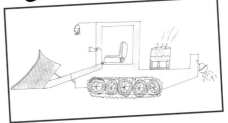

Niall, aged 11

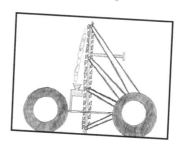

Felix, aged 11

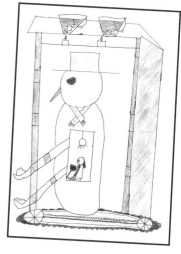

Sophie, aged 11

- Draw a sketch of your machine.
- Use the sketch as a starting point for making your model.
- When your model is complete, paint it all over.

This model was made from a plastic tub and cardboard tubes with bottle tops for wheels.

Sophia and Eleanor, both aged 11

Jasmine, aged 10

This model was made from a plastic bottle with a handle, and wooden circles on thin dowels for wheels.

This model was made from a cardboard box, with drink cans for wheels and a yogurt pot for the funnel.

Niall and William, both aged 11

Clothes chooser

Design a machine to choose clothes for you, whatever the weather.

◉ Draw a sketch to show how the machine might work.

Eleanor, aged 11

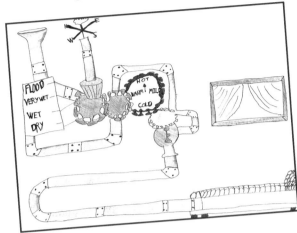

Sophia, aged 11

◉ Make a model of your machine.

Arty tips

✰ Use cardboard rolls, plastic bottles and lids, clean yogurt pots, straws and cardboard cartons and boxes for model-making.

✰ If you want to paint your model, use glue instead of sticky tape or the paint won't stay.

✰ To attach revolving parts, such as wheels or cogs, push a split pin through the centre.

Sophia and Eleanor, both aged 11

ARTISTS AND ANSWERS

WHATEVER THE WEATHER (pages 4/5)

ABOUT HENRI ROUSSEAU

Rousseau (1844-1910) was a self-taught French painter. He served in the army and then worked as a customs officer in Paris. After he retired, he painted portraits, scenes of everyday life and flowers, as well as imaginary, dream-like scenes, set in exotic surroundings.

ABOUT CHARLES BURCHFIELD

Burchfield (1893-1967) was born in Ohio, USA. As a child, he was fascinated by the shapes, sounds and smells of nature. After studying art in New York, he moved to Buffalo and painted city scenes. Later, he painted mainly landscapes, showing his awe of nature by using bold shapes, patterns and colours.

SUNNY DAYS (pages 6/7)

Answers for page 6

• *Hockney used strongly contrasting colours, which look extra bright when seen side by side. Monet used a narrow range of pale colours to give a feeling of coldness and soft light.*
• *Hockney used darker shades of pink and blue to show the shadows on the building and the side of the swimming pool. Monet used cool blues and greys for the shadows of the fence and the gate.*

ABOUT DAVID HOCKNEY

Hockney (born 1937) is an English artist who first became known as a painter. He is particularly famous for his portraits and interiors, which use strong, flat colours with a focus on light and reflections. He has also done stage designs for ballets and operas, made films, experimented with photomontages, fax art and computer prints, and created many book illustrations.

Answers for page 7

• *The white paint indicates the splash made by a hidden diver.*
• *The smooth, flat scenery makes the splash stand out.*
• *The long, pale shadows show that it is early morning.*
• *The magpie provides both a sign of life and a point of focus. It is hard to judge the scale of the picture without it.*

ABOUT CLAUDE MONET

Monet (1840-1926) grew up on the north coast of France. A local artist encouraged him to paint out in the open air, instead of indoors in a studio as most other painters did. Monet then moved to Paris and befriended other artists, such as Alfred Sisley, Pierre-Auguste Renoir and Camille Pissarro. He persuaded them to them to paint outdoors as well. They developed a style known as Impressionism, named after one of Monet's paintings.

FUN ON THE ICE (pages 10/11)

ABOUT HENDRIK AVERCAMP

Avercamp (1585-1634) grew up deaf and mute in Kampen, Holland, where he lived for most of his life. He became famous for his wintry scenes of sports and activities on ice. He sketched the figures from life and then worked them into paintings in his studio.

WALKING IN THE RAIN (pages 14/15)

Answers for page 14

• Caillebotte used pale, drab yellows and browns, and a range of cold greys and blues, to suggest a rainy day.
• People are dressed in warm clothes and some look hunched, suggesting that it might be chilly as well as wet. The cool colours add to the effect.
• The figures look detached, isolated and perhaps lonely.

ABOUT GUSTAVE CAILLEBOTTE

Caillebotte (1848-1894) came from a wealthy Parisian family. He gave up a career in law to concentrate on painting. He befriended the Impressionists, including Monet, Renoir and Alfred Sisley, and helped to organise their exhibitions and support them with funds. He painted mainly scenes of modern Paris, interiors, bathers and boats.

FEELING THE HEAT (pages 18/19)

Answers for page 19

• *Thick, broken brushstrokes suggest rippling water.*
• *The bare parts of the canvas suggest that the glare of the sunlight makes the water impossible to see.*
• *The blue outline makes the figure stand out.*

ABOUT ANDRÉ DERAIN

Derain (1880-1954) was born in Chatou, near Paris. He studied painting and became friends with the artist Henri Matisse. They both painted views of Chatou, Pecq and Collioure in the south of France. Derain also painted pictures of London. He and other like-minded artists were given the nickname 'Fauves' (meaning wild beasts) because of their unusual use of vivid, unrealistic colours.

BLOWING IN THE WIND (pages 22/23)

Answers for page 22

• *People's clothes are shown pushed against their bodies and lifting into the air, demonstrating the force of the wind.*
• *The wind is blowing from the left of the picture. You can tell this because the trees and people are leaning to the right.*
• *The grass is also windblown.*
• *The mountain, Mount Fuji, and the other hill in the distance provide a still contrast to the windy scene.*

ABOUT HOKUSAI

Hokusai (1760-1849) was a Japanese print-maker. When he was young he learned painting and book illustration. He then designed *surimono* – small decorated prints for invitations, announcements or greetings. He is well known for his views of Mount Fuji, the highest mountain in Japan, and also his bright woodblock prints of actors and dancers.

Answers for page 23

• *The wind is blowing from the right in Renoir's painting.*
• *The white patches might be areas with more sunlight shining on them. The picture looks duller and colder without them.*

ABOUT PIERRE-AUGUSTE RENOIR

Renoir (1841-1919) was born in Limoges, France. After working as a painter of porcelain and blinds, he studied at the *Ecole des Beaux-Arts in Paris*. He painted Impressionist landscapes with Monet, but later preferred to paint portraits and people at the theatre, in dance halls or on country outings.

WACKY WEATHER (pages 26/27)

Answers for page 27

• *Spray marks above the funnel show rain collecting.*
• *The three cyclists at the back power the broom.*
• *The front cyclist makes the snow scooper turn.*
• *The snow drops into a hanging pot. The flame under the pot melts the snow and turns it into steam.*
• *One man is the lookout; another blows a whistle to keep the cyclists pedalling in time; the others survey the scene.*
• *The roller smoothes the swept ground.*
• *The driver has a horn to warn people that he's coming.*

ABOUT WILLIAM HEATH ROBINSON

Heath Robinson (1872-1944) was a British illustrator. His early book illustrations included *The Pilgrim's Progress, Tales from Shakespeare and Andersen's Fairy Tales*. His later comic illustrations featured ingenious, wacky gadgets for improving people's lifestyles, and funny household scenes.

GLOSSARY

atmosphere The feeling or mood of a place.

canvas A stiff cloth that artists use to paint on.

collage A picture made by sticking bits of paper, fabric, or other objects, on to a background.

cool colours Shades of blue, grey and green that give a chilly feel.

Fauves A group of artists who painted using bold, unrealistic colours to express different feelings.

glaze A shiny coating.

hot (or warm) colours Shades of red, yellow and orange that have a warm glow.

Impressionists A group of artists who painted out in the open air and focused on the effects of light.

landscape A countryside scene.

studio An artist's or photographer's workplace.

texture How something feels to the touch, for example rough or smooth.

INDEX

Paintings are shown in bold

animals 5, 11
atmosphere 12, 32
Avercamp, Hendrik 10, 11, 12, 30

A Bigger Splash 6, 30
Boats in the Port of Collioure 18–19, 31
brushstrokes 19, 23
Burchfield, Charles 5, 17, 24, 30

Caillebotte, Gustave 14, 30, 31

canvas 5, 19, 31, 32
clouds 11, 23
clothes 12, 17, 22, 25, 27, 29, 30, 31
collage 8, 17, 32
colours 6, 7, 9, 11, 13, 14, 16, 17, 19, 20, 21, 24, 30, 31, 32

Derain, André 19, 21, 31

Eriji in Suruga Province (A Sudden Gust of Wind) 22, 31

Fauves 31, 32

glaze 5, 32
The Gust of Wind 23, 31

Heath Robinson, William 27, 31
Hockney, David 6, 9, 30
Hokusai 22, 31

ice 10–11, 12, 30
imaginary scenes 5, 29, 30
Impressionism 30, 31, 32

landscapes 9, 21, 23, 24, 30
Late Winter Radiance 5, 30
light 4, 9, 21, 30, 32
lightning 5

The Magpie 7, 30
Monet, Claude 7, 21, 24, 30, 31
movement 7, 22, 23

A New Snow-plough for Clearing a Footpath after a Heavy Fall 27, 31

Paris 5, 14, 30, 31
Paris Street, Rainy Day 14–15, 30
people 10, 11, 12, 13, 14, 16, 17, 19, 22, 25, 27, 28, 30, 31

rain 4, 5, 14–15, 16, 17, 27, 30, 31
reflections 10, 17, 30
Renoir, Pierre-Auguste 23, 30, 31
Rousseau, Henri 4, 5, 17, 30

seasons 5, 13
shadows 6, 9, 14, 30
sky 5, 9, 10, 13, 19, 23
snow 7, 9, 12, 13, 27, 28, 31
storm 5
studio 30, 32
summer 13, 19
sun 4, 5, 6–7, 9, 19, 31

texture 8, 17, 32
Tiger in a Tropical Storm (Surprised!) 4, 17, 30
trees 5, 7, 9, 10, 11, 12, 13, 22, 23

umbrellas 14, 16, 25

weather machines 26–29, 31
weathervane 27
weaving 20
What Shall I Put On? 26, 31
wind 4, 5, 22–23, 24, 25, 27, 31
winter 5, 7, 9, 10–11, 12, 30
Winter Landscape with Ice Skaters 10–11, 30